BOOTS AND BANDAGES

by

Jane Holderness-Roddam

Illustrations by

Carole Vincer

THRESHOLD BOOKS

First published in Great Britain by
Threshold Books Limited, 661 Fulham Road,
London SW6 5PZ

© Threshold Books Limited 1987.

Typeset by Falcon Graphic Art Ltd,
Wallington, Surrey
Printed in Italy by
New Interlitho, Milan

ISBN 0–901366–33–1

CONTENTS

4   Introduction

BOOTS   5   Over-reach boots
6   Fetlock boots
7   Brushing boots
8   Competition boots
9   Travelling boots
10   Knee caps
11   Hock boots
12   Fastenings
14   Care and storage of boots

BANDAGES   15   Types of bandage
16   Bandages
18   Putting on a tail bandage
19   Removing bandages
20   Bandaging an injured knee
21   Bandaging an injured hock
22   Bandaging an injured foot
23   Sewing and taping bandages
24   Care and storage of bandages

Introduction

There is a wide variety of boots and bandages on the market today, designed to protect a horse's leg from the knee and hock joint down to the hoof. The more traditional bandage when correctly applied gives unrivalled support, whilst boots, made from materials such as leather, felt, plastic or rubber, are quick and easy to put on and provide a protective shell round any specific part of the limb which is prone to injury.

Shoeing plays an important part in a horse's way of going, and often a discussion with the blacksmith will be far more beneficial than indiscriminate use of boots. However, prevention is always better than cure, and protecting your horse from injury with an appropriate boot or bandage may prevent an unnecessary and expensive call to the vet.

Most boots are designed with extra padding around the spot that they are aiming to protect, and should be chosen carefully with this in mind. As they must be robust enough to withstand inevitable wear and tear, a more expensive design is often preferable to the many cheap and flimsy ones which often split after just a couple of uses. When choosing bandages, check that they are long enough, have strong enough tapes or Velcro, and are of good quality.

The following pages set out to explain in a simple, easy to follow way how and when to fit and use the most common boots and bandages, paying special attention to the distinctive features of each type.

Over-reach boots

Over-reach or bell boots are designed to protect the heels of the front legs from being trodden on.
They should be used for all jumping or fast work. Rubber ones are best and can be softened in hot water if stiff to pull on. Buckles can cause a horse to stumble should he tread on them.

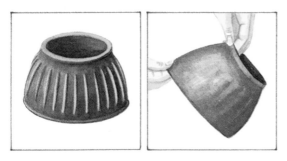

Turn the boot inside out, support the foreleg and pull the boot over the foot.

Lower the foot and turn the boot the right way round.

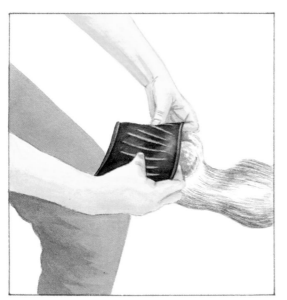

To remove, face forwards, rest the toe on your knee, and pull the boot towards you, over the heel. Support the foot so that it does not knock the opposite leg.

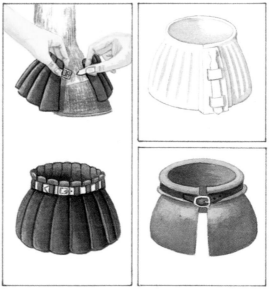

Some over-reach boots buckle around the pastern. The straps must be secured with keepers. The petal boot has replaceable petals in case of damage.

Fetlock boots

The fetlock joints are very vulnerable to knocks, especially on the hind legs, as many horses move extremely close behind. Once bruised, the joint can become chronically enlarged from continuous friction unless it is protected. The simple **Yorkshire boot** made from woollen material and fastened with a wide tape can solve the problem. If just one leg is knocked, one boot will be sufficient; if both, a pair of more substantial **fetlock boots** will be preferable and will last longer.

The **sausage boot** made of thick rubber tubing threaded on a strap is fitted to the pastern of one hind leg. It will protect the pastern or coronet if this is prone to injury, such as a jumper striking himself as he takes off at an obstacle.

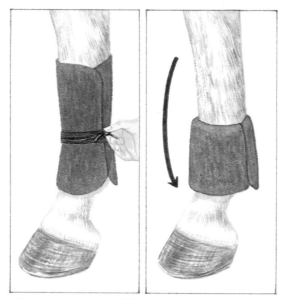

Yorkshire boots With the wider portion uppermost, fold around the leg and tie the tapes flat on the outside. Pull the top portion down over the lower one.

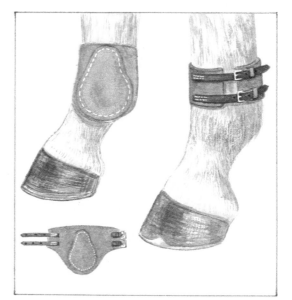

Fetlock boots Fasten just above the fetlock joint, and slide down into a comfortable position. Adjust so that they cannot rotate. Slot straps in keepers.

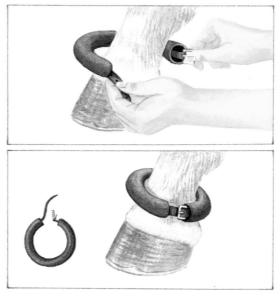

Sausage boot Buckle the boot around the hind pastern. Push the strap tongue inside the tube to secure it. Tape over the buckle for extra security.

Brushing boots

Moving up the leg to the cannon bone, there is a wide choice of boots to suit different types of work and to provide the protection required by your particular horse.

A full-length **brushing boot** will protect the leg from the knee joint to the fetlock. The best designs offer strength, softness and security. **Speedicut boots**, cut high on the inside, will protect the high stepping horse or jumper who tends to strike himself.

Tendon boots, designed to withstand a strike into the front tendon, have extra padding down the back, often with an added supportive sorbo rubber strip lying on either side of the tendons. **Tendon moulds** can also be put inside brushing boots, or bandaged into place for extra protection.

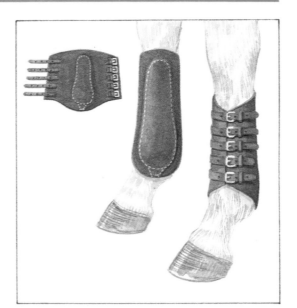

A plain leather **brushing boot** to protect cannon bone and fetlock joint. It is lined with sorbo rubber for softness, with straps and buckles evenly spaced to secure it.

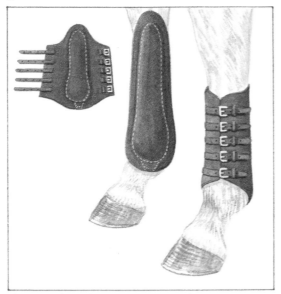

A **speedicut boot** to protect the vulnerable inside of the hock. A similar style used in front will protect the inside of the knee.

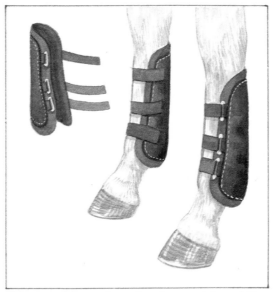

An open-fronted **tendon boot** with padding down the back and support strips on the inside. The Velcro straps loop through metal eyes then press back on themselves.

Competition boots

A **competition boot** must give good protection and have secure fastenings, as the horse could stumble if the boot came undone. As weight is also a consideration, a non-absorbent boot is most suitable if water has to be negotiated.

Open-fronted boots are popular with show jumpers as they protect the tendons but leave the front of the leg clear.

Polo boots are very well padded to absorb accidental blows in the course of a game, and are probably the best protection on the market, as they are designed to come well down over the fetlock joint. However, since they are bulky, absorbent and become heavy when wet, they are not suitable for eventing or long-distance riding.

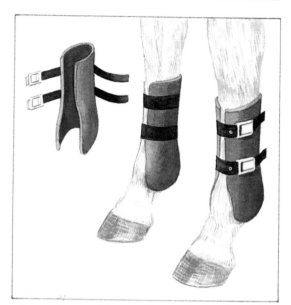

Open-fronted boot. Fit to the back of the tendons on the forelegs, fastenings to the outside, not the front. The moulding should rest comfortably on the leg.

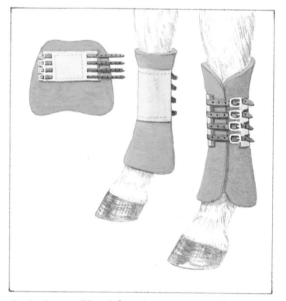

Polo boot. Used for close-moving horses, lungeing, or polo. Fasten the middle buckle first, then the top and bottom ones. As these boots are bulky, check that they are secure.

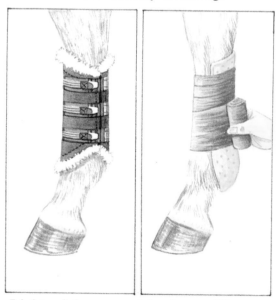

Lightweight competition boots. These give good protection, as well as being very light. Tendon moulds should be bandaged firmly but not above or below the mould.

Travelling boots

Travelling boots are quick and easy to fit and give adequate protection in a box or trailer. There are several types, mostly made of synthetic materials lined with foam, fleece or cotton and fastened with Velcro. Some are designed to protect the whole lower leg including the knees and hocks; others are shorter.

For long distances or a very twisty journey, travelling boots do not give as good support as bandages. For the same reason many people prefer to use bandages on the homeward journey from a competition.

Bandages may also be more appropriate for a bad traveller, as the Velcro on boots can come undone if the horse thrashes around. Boots can be fitted on top of bandages for extra protection, and taped in place to hold them firmly.

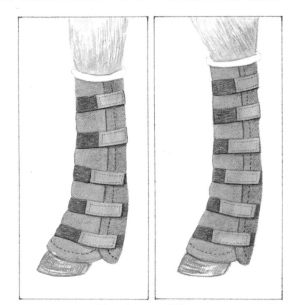

Short travelling boots. The top straps fasten first, from front to back. If used, knee caps and hock boots should be put on afterwards.

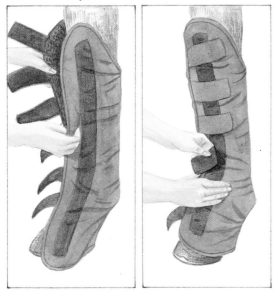

Long travelling boots. Hold the boot behind the leg and fasten the tapes firmly without pulling them too tightly across the joints.

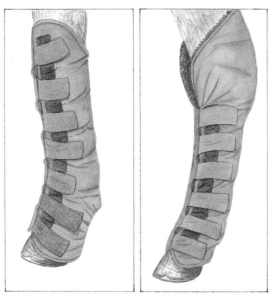

The boots should be high enough to cover the knees and hocks adequately and should reach down over the coronet. Remember that hoof oil will soil the boots.

Knee caps

The knee joint is very vulnerable to knocks and bruising, so protection is important. **Travelling knee caps** are a sensible investment and the **skeleton pattern** a useful precaution for road work. These can also be used for horses with chronic 'big knees' who tend to knock themselves when jumping.

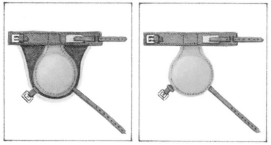

The bulkier **travelling knee cap** (left) and the lighter **exercise pad**. Both have elasticated inserts, to give flexibility to the top buckle, and long lower straps.

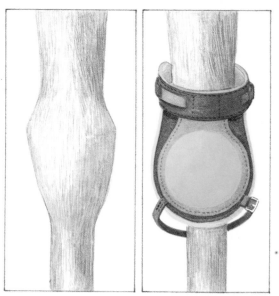

The front view of the knee demonstrates where the knee cap should rest above the prominent knee bone.

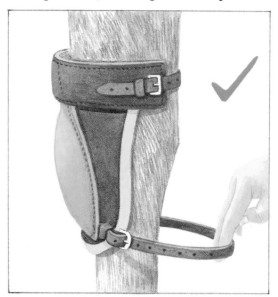

The correct application of a knee cap. The lower strap is fastened loosely to allow free movement of the knee joint, essential if the horse is not to stumble.

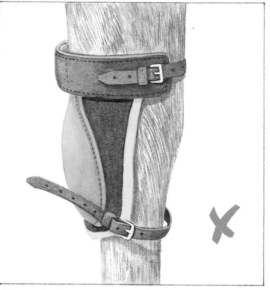

Here the lower strap is far too tight. When the knee is flexed it will restrict the movement, possibly resulting in a fall, and chafe the back of the knee.

Hock boots

Like the knee, the hock is prone to injury on journeys, or in the stable if there is insufficient bedding. Once damaged, the hock can become chronically swollen or 'capped', causing intermittent trouble.

Hock boots should be kept soft and well oiled and must be well padded inside. They should not be left on for long periods, such as in the stable, where extra bedding ought to guard adequately against injury.

A long **travelling boot** is perhaps better designed for hock protection as it has no fastening to create pressure round the joint. As with the knee cap, the hock boots are fastened securely by the top strap whilst the lower one remains loose to allow free movement.

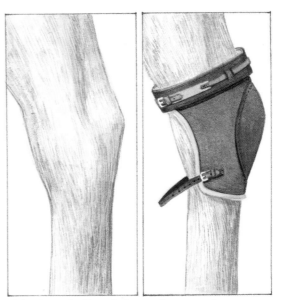

The boot is fitted above the prominent bones of the joint and protects the point of the hock. Buckles must fasten on the outside of the joint.

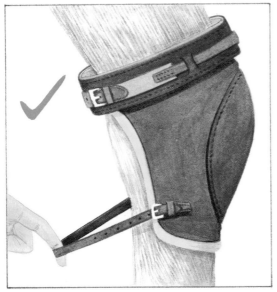

The lower strap must be fastened loosely to allow free movement and to avoid pressure on the hock. Elastic on the top strap gives slight flexibility.

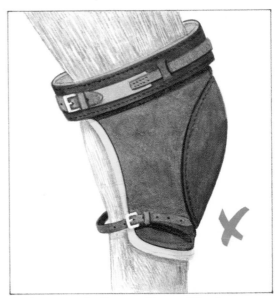

An incorrectly fastened boot. The lower strap will create pressure on the hock and severely restrict movement. It is liable to rub and cause pressure sores.

Fastenings

Boots are normally fastened by Velcro, clips or buckles, the latter two being the most secure. **Velcro**, although excellent when new, quickly loses its effectiveness if it becomes clogged with dirt or fluff. To maintain its self-gripping properties it must be 'de-fluffed' regularly by hand or with a darning needle. Many boots have double Velcro fastenings for extra security. Adhesive tape applied on top of the Velcro at the same tension will also help to secure it, but is not a very effective long-term method.

   Clip fastenings are fairly secure. They should fasten from the front of the boot to the back and are often combined with a Velcro strip, running from back to front beneath them. Some clips are fixed to pieces of strong elastic but beware of boots that are too tight or small for the horse; they could strain the clips and hinder circulation.

   Buckles are the most satisfactory fastening as long as they are kept soft and pliable. The keepers must be in good condition, otherwise the boots could come undone. Buckles should always be fastened on the outside of the leg, with the points of the straps towards the back to avoid becoming caught up as the horse moves forward. They must be fastened securely enough to hold the boot in place, starting with one of the middle straps and finishing with the lower one, which must not hinder the movement of the fetlock joint. If the buckles are fixed to elastic this may become progressively longer as it slackens with wear.

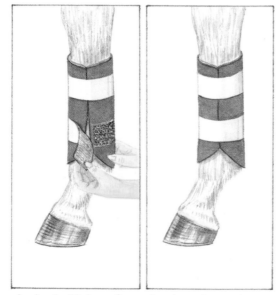 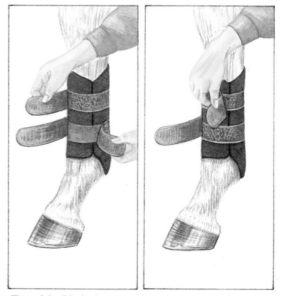

A **single Velcro** fastening is quite adequate for ordinary riding. It is quick and easy to apply, and effective until the Velcro becomes clogged up.

Double Velcro, though bulky, is a much more secure fastening and is suitable for competitions. Inner tapes fasten from back to front, top tapes front to back.

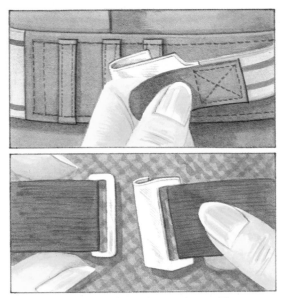

Two designs of **metal fastenings**. *Top*: a clip and plastic eye, usually used with Velcro for extra strength. *Bottom*: metal clip and eye on elasticated strap.

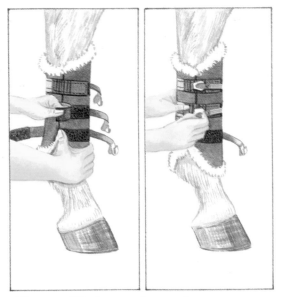

Clips and Velcro make good secure fastenings. The Velcro is fastened from back to front with the clips on top from front to back.

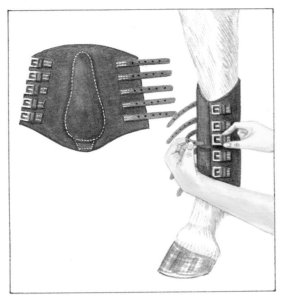

Plain buckles are very secure. They should hold the boot securely but not too tightly or they might restrict the movement or circulation.

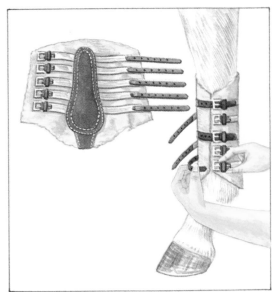

Some buckles are attached to **elasticated straps** for extra support. Care must be taken not to pull the straps too tight, causing uneven pressure.

Care and storage of boots

It is essential to keep boots scrupulously clean and supple. They can easily rub the horse, creating a sore or infection if they are not kept in good condition. Regular care will also prolong their life considerably.

Immediately after use, all boots should be rubbed off and dried if necessary. Leather parts should be soaped well and oiled periodically to keep them in good shape. To save endless washing, which is not always best for the boot, allow caked dirt to dry, then brush the insides with a stiff brush.

Many boots can be washed quite safely in a machine, though Velcro fastenings should be fitted together first to stop them becoming clogged with fluff and other dirt during the wash. Once dry, use a darning needle to 'de-fluff' the Velcro.

Tendon moulds should be washed in warm soapy water as necessary and then allowed to dry naturally.

Before boots are stored for any period of time it is essential to clean them thoroughly. Soap or apply Vaseline to the leather, and pack with moth balls if any parts of the boots are made of felt or wool.

As buckles tend to cause wear on the leather straps, it is important to check them regularly and to send them to the saddler for repair at the first sign of deterioration.

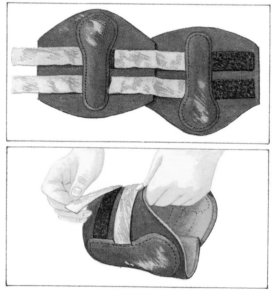

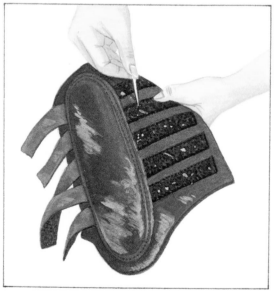

Velcro fastenings taped together before washing in a machine. Make sure that the boots are completely dry before putting them away.

A quick and easy fastening, Velcro will soon become useless unless kept clean. A darning needle is an excellent tool for removing fluff and dirt.

Types of bandage

Stable and travelling bandages are made of **wool** for warmth and thickness. Some are designed for use without additional padding.

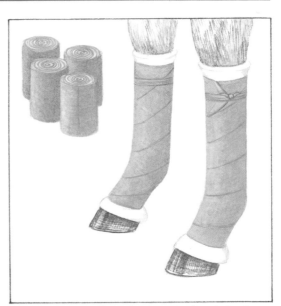

Crèpe is excellent for bandaging injuries as it will easily mould to all shapes. It is also popular as a support bandage for competitions.

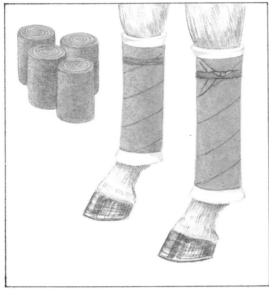

Stockinette bandages made of **cotton** are easy to wash and useful in the stable or for travelling. Cooler than wool, they are suitable for hot conditions.

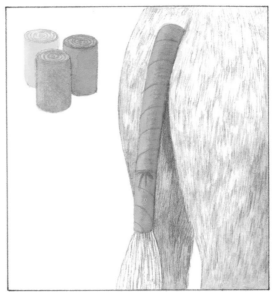

There is a variety of **elasticated** bandages for tails. Choose a medium-stretch type as they can restrict the circulation if the elastication is too strong.

Bandages

Bandages are an essential part of a stable's equipment, and are used for protection, support and warmth, as well as for the care of injuries. Applying a bandage is an art which can only be perfected with practice. However, unless it is done well it can easily result in injury to the horse, so it is very important to know the pitfalls.

The secret of good bandaging lies in correct and even tension. Always begin with the bandages firmly and evenly rolled up. A good basis of gamgee or a similar cotton or foam backed padding is also essential. The bandage must be long enough to reach from just below the knee or hock down the leg and back again in even turns. Many bandages are far too short, except for ponies, so check the length before buying. A bandage cannot give adequate protection if it does not cover the leg properly.

Leg bandages are all applied in basically the same way, though those used for support need to be firmer than ones put on for warmth. An exercise bandage should reach down on to the fetlock joint without hindering the movement. A stable bandage should cover the pastern. When tying the tapes, make sure that they are the same tension as the rest of the bandage – neither tighter nor slacker.

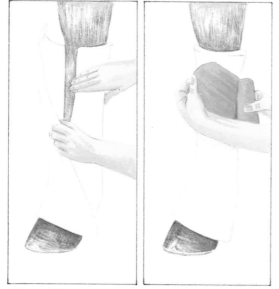

Travelling or stable bandages. Gamgee or other protective padding is essential to guard against knocks or pressure. Wrap around the leg, as shown.

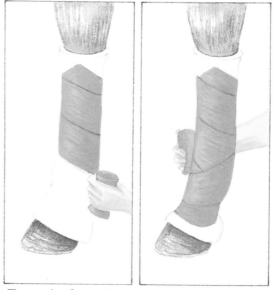

From the front, bandage anti-clockwise down the leg and as far over the joint as possible, for greatest protection, before turning back up the leg.

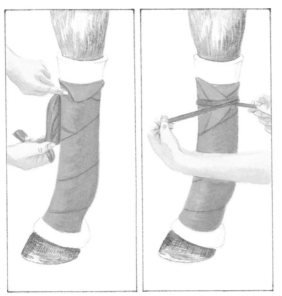

The length of the bandage will determine the depth of each turn. Aim to finish back at the beginning of the bandage to secure the tip before tying the tapes.

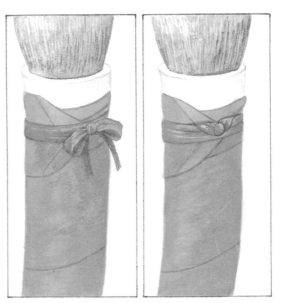

Keep tapes flat and secure with a firm knot tucked into the bandage on the outside. Never tie on the back or front of the leg, as this can injure it.

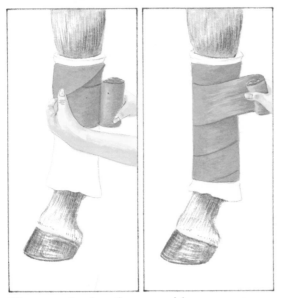

The **exercise bandage** provides support and protection when riding or competing. It should reach on to, but not over, the fetlock.

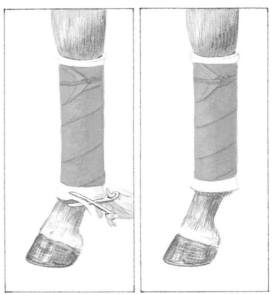

Protruding padding should be trimmed, and tapes fastened on the outside and tucked into the bandage. Make sure that the tension is even throughout.

Putting on a tail bandage

Bandaging a tail well requires practice, but there is no doubt that some horses' tails are much easier to bandage than others. Start by damping the tail (not the bandage, which will shrink as it dries) with a little water to give grip. Position the bandage well up under the dock as shown, and proceed in firm, even turns down the tail almost to the tip of the dock, then back up again. Tie the tapes flat on top of the tail, about halfway down the bandage. To finish, curve the tail into a natural shape.

Some tail bandages are very stretchy, and it is important not to pull them too tight and hinder the circulation. The tapes should be tied no tighter than the bandage, and bandages should never be left on overnight; either could seriously damage the tail.

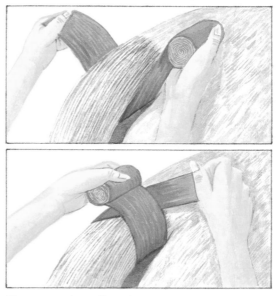

Dampen the tail and start the bandage well up under the dock. Take a firm, even turn, leaving the end of the bandage loose as a flap.

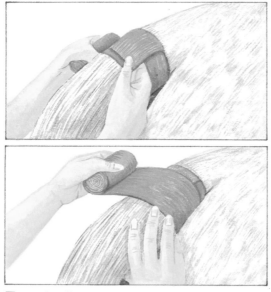

Turn the flap down and secure with one complete turn before continuing down the tail, making sure each turn is not too tight.

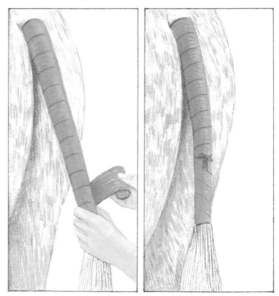

Bandage almost to the end of the dock then return with even turns. Fasten the tapes flat around the tail with the knot on top.

18

Removing bandages

Leg bandages

Begin by undoing the knot or Velcro that fastens the bandage then pass it quickly from hand to hand as you unwrap each turn. Do not try to fold or roll the bandage as you unwind it, this will only result in a crooked roll and will tend to pull the leg. Remove the padding and massage the legs lightly but briskly with your hands, checking that all is well. Never kneel on the ground to deal with bandages, as any sudden movement from the horse will leave you in a very vulnerable position.

Bandages should be aired and, if necessary, brushed off quickly before you roll them ready for use again. Brush or shake out the padding to keep it fresh.

Tail bandages

This is quick and effortless, but some horses can be a little apprehensive if it is done too hurriedly. The tail is very sensitive and a horse will remember careless handling and be less cooperative next time.

Undo the tapes then ease the bandage gently from the top of the dock. Slide it down the tail to the end, in short pulls, without trying to unwrap it. A very full tail might be too bulky to allow you to do this, in which case you will have to undo the bandage completely.

Never leave a tail bandage on all night, as the tapes might restrict the circulation and cause permanent damage to the tail.

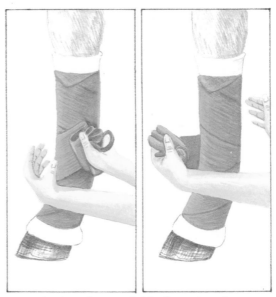

Pass the bandage quickly from hand to hand as you unwrap it. Keep both feet on the ground and *crouch* to do this; it is dangerous to kneel.

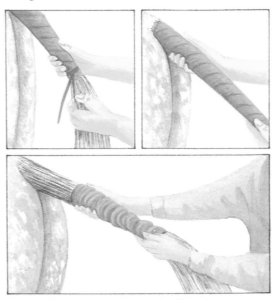

Undo the tapes and ease the bandage down the dock, then pull it right down and over the end of the tail. Once clear, unravel and re-roll it.

Bandaging an injured knee

The knee is not an easy joint to bandage, as it is, by nature, very flexible and its prominent bones are very vulnerable to pressure. Apart from the injury itself, the most sensitive point is the bone at the back of the knee. If a bandage restricts the circulation at this point even a minor knee injury could become severe.

Plenty of padding around the knee is essential. The figure-of-eight method of bandaging leaves the back of the knee free from pressure and allows adequate movement. Standard stable bandages should always be applied for support before the knee is bandaged.

As every case is different, the following method should be treated as a basic guide rather than a hard and fast rule.

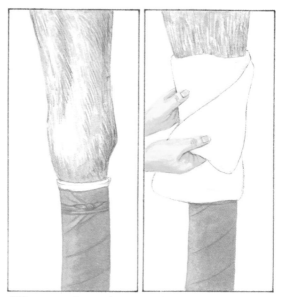

The prominent bone at the back of the knee is vulnerable to pressure. Apply stable bandages then plenty of padding round the knee to secure the dressing.

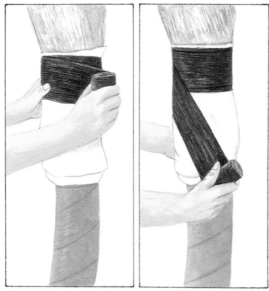

Make a few firm turns above the joint. Cross down over the front or side. Make two or three more turns below the knee, then cross up the front again.

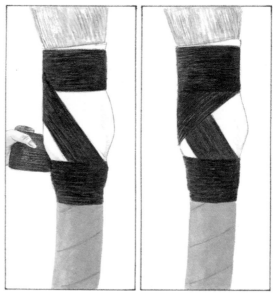

Repeat figure-of-eight as necessary. Keep bandage clear of prominent bone at back. Check that padding does not slip. A second bandage may be required on top.

Bandaging an injured hock

Start by bandaging both hind legs for support and to help keep the hock bandage in place when it is applied. The prominent bone on the inside of the hock is vulnerable to pressure, so take care to avoid it.

Use a large roll of gamgee to pad both above and below the joint. Bandage a couple of turns above the hock, cross over the front, take a few turns below and over the stable bandage then take the bandage up the leg again in front of the hock. Check that it does not press on the prominent bone and that the point of the hock is well protected. Two bandages may be necessary.

As hock dressings have a tendency to slip down as the horse moves an Elastoplast bandage around the top part of the leg and bandage will help to hold it in place.

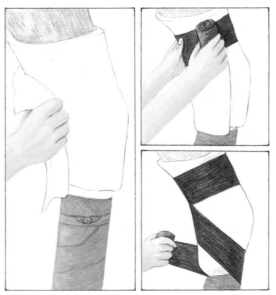

Apply stable bandages, then plenty of padding around the whole area. Start above the hock then take a turn down in front, avoiding the prominent bone on the inside.

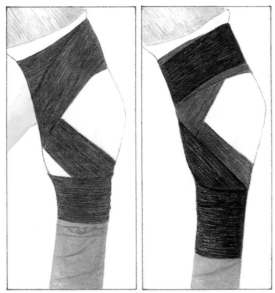

Repeat the figure-of-eight, taking turns above and below to hold everything in position. Secure the tapes below the hock and apply Elastoplast to prevent slipping.

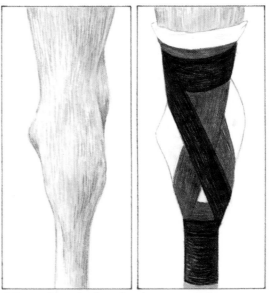

View of hock showing bony prominence on inside. The method of bandaging shown on the right avoids pressure which could cause damage.

Bandaging an injured foot

Foot bandages applied over dressings are difficult to keep in place for any length of time. The secret lies in using plenty of padding and applying a firm bandage on top.

As always, apply stable bandages first. Put the poultice or dressing on the foot, and cover it with plastic and a good wad of padding. This must be wide enough to bandage over completely, so that none may be pulled out from underneath. Place a strong piece of plastic or a corner of a clean industrial plastic bag over the foot and begin the bandage firmly round the pastern. Turn it in a figure-of-eight pattern round and over the foot several times before finishing the bandage up the leg once more.

A bib may be required if the horse tries to chew the dressing.

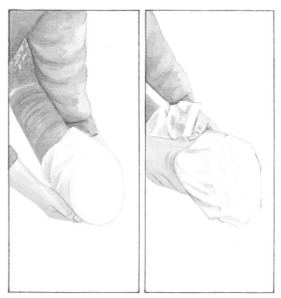

After poulticing the foot, cover it with plastic and a large thick piece of padding. Put a thick, strong plastic bag or the corner of a hessian sack on top.

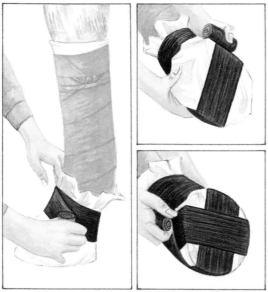

With the foot on the ground to hold the padding and plastic, apply an elasticated bandage to the pastern, then cross it in a figure-of-eight over and around the foot.

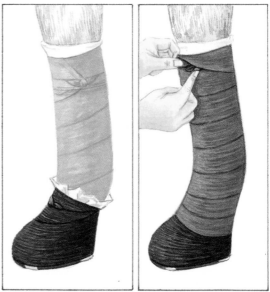

A second bandage may well be necessary. Take it up over the stable bandage. Make sure that all tapes are tucked well away so that the horse does not play with them.

Sewing and taping bandages

Sewing and taping are both ways of making bandages more secure, especially for competitions where a fall caused by a loose bandage could make the difference between winning and losing.

Bandages with tapes should be tied as before, and the finished, well-tightened knot stitched through at the top and bottom.

Self-adhesive bandages or ones without tapes should be stitched in a careful criss-cross on the outside of the leg.

Tendons can easily be damaged if tapes or adhesive are pulled too tight and hinder circulation. They should be the same tension as the rest of the bandage; never tighter. Taping tends to come undone in the wet but it is quite effective in dry conditions.

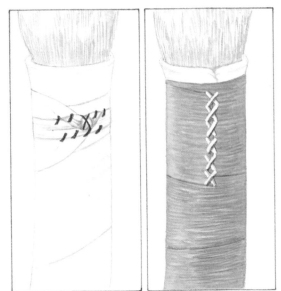

Two kinds of bandage secured by stitching. Knot and tapes, *left*, are sewn over and, *right*, a bandage without tapes is neatly stitched down its edge.

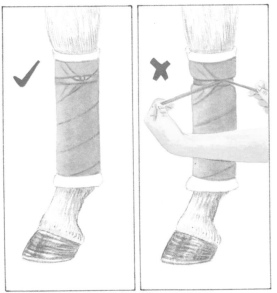

The right and wrong way to tie tapes. *Left*: the tapes are the same tension as the bandage. *Right*: they are pulled too tight and press on the tendons.

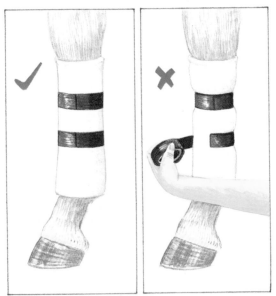

When taping, the same principles apply. The tape should be no tighter than the rest of the bandage. Uneven pressure can damage the leg.

Care and storage of bandages

Bandages need to be kept in good condition if they are to last. Woollen bandages should be brushed or shaken thoroughly after every use. If they are to be stored for any length of time, they should be washed and dried well then packed with moth balls.

Elasticated and stockinette bandages will need more frequent washing. If they are washed in a machine they should be put in a bag to prevent tangling, although hand washing will double their lifespan. Coloured bandages may not be colour-fast, so should be washed separately.

Flatten tapes while they are still damp, and re-stitch if necessary before they become detached. Velcro fastenings must be 'de-fluffed' regularly if they are to stay effective.

Gamgee should be replaced as necessary when it becomes worn. Some people blanket-stitch around the edges to prolong its life. Most other paddings can be washed or brushed to keep them clean and fresh. Rubber-backed padding tends to make the legs sweat, and therefore disintegrates more quickly, so it is best washed by hand to avoid deterioration.

When buying bandages look for a suitable length and width, with wide tapes which will be less likely to pull tight and cause pressure than narrow ones.

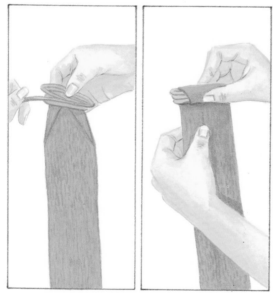

To roll a bandage, flatten and fold the tapes and roll in towards them so they will lie flat when applied. With Velcro fastenings, roll in towards the fluffy side.

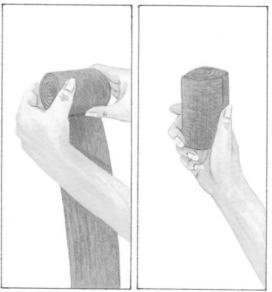

Roll firmly and evenly, keeping the bandage straight or it will be impossible to re-apply effectively.